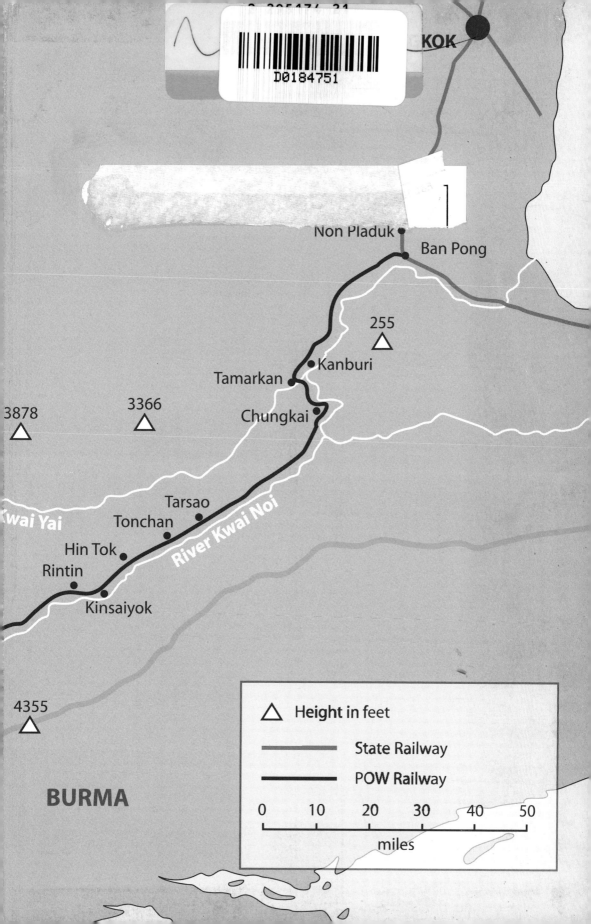

KOK

Non Pladuk

Ban Pong

255

Kanburi

Tamarkan

3366

Chungkai

3878

Tarsao

Kwai Yai

Tonchan

River Kwai Noi

Hin Tok

Rintin

Kinsaiyok

4355

BURMA

△ Height in feet

——— State Railway

——— POW Railway

0   10   20   30   40   50

miles

ARTHUR GODMAN

THE
WILL
TO
SURVIVE

with illustrations by
RONALD SEARLE
and
PHILIP MENINSKY

SPELLMOUNT

STAPLEHURST

© 2002 Arthur Godman 2 295174 21

British Library Cataloguing in Publication Data:
A catalogue record for this book is available
from the British Library.

ISBN 1-86227-111-9

Published in the UK in 2002 by
Spellmount Limited
The Old Rectory
Staplehurst
Kent TN12 0AZ

1 3 5 7 9 8 6 4 2

Set in Photina
Designed and produced by
Pardoe Blacker Publishing Limited
Lingfield · Surrey

Printed in the United Kingdom
by Compass Press

Contents

List of illustrations

Introduction

THIS STORY actually starts in Changi, a small area on the north-eastern tip of Singapore island. How had I come to live in this area and under alien circumstances?

The chain of events which led to my living in Changi began way before the start of the Second World War. I had finished at University College, University of London, at the end of July 1939, and had left with a first class honours degree in chemistry. While at the university I had joined the Officers' Training Corps (OTC) and had become an instructor in sound ranging, having passed all my OTC examinations. In 1937 I joined the Reserve of Officers, and when war was declared in September 1939, I was instructed to report for duty immediately.

As there appeared to be little demand for sound rangers I was sent on a short course for artillery officers, and then posted to a territorial regiment in January 1940. I did not have long to wait in England; in March the regiment was sent to France. After a period of training the war began in earnest on the 10 May 1940 and the regiment was despatched with Third Corps to defend Belgium.

We held a defensive position near Oudenarde in Belgium, and I was in charge of the command post for one of the two batteries in the regiment, organizing battery targets. When the Germans attacked, the position was maintained for four days – with some difficulty as our guns were Mark II 18-pounders that the army had discarded in 1916 (being replaced by Mark IV guns). We were withdrawn as field gunners and became anti-tank gunners, with moderate success.

With the army in retreat we fell back towards Dunkirk, where I reached the beaches late in the evening, with about a dozen men. These were from my small anti-tank hunting unit that had lost contact with the rest of the battery. We queued on a small pier for embarking on a destroyer, but missed it by six men. It was full and pulled away – but luck was on our side because the destroyer was heavily shelled out in the harbour.

After a day on the beach at Dunkirk I joined a queue wading out to the launches, climbed aboard a small motor boat that pulled away out into the harbour and then ran aground. As the tide rose we luckily floated off the sand bank, and I eventually climbed aboard a Dutch coastal vessel. This took us to Ramsgate, where we disembarked and were taken by train to a camp to be sorted out into our army formations.

*　　　　*　　　　*

Feeling restless in England I volunteered for a draft to go to Iraq, but never reached there. At Bombay, I was taken off the troopship and posted to a regiment in Nowshera, a town in the North West Frontier Province of what was then India but is now Pakistan. I was twenty-four years old when I arrived in India – with some experience of actual fighting in a war. The North West Frontier was guarded by three army brigades, with the Nowshera brigade being one of the three. Our duties included the general guarding of the Khyber Pass and the frontier, and acting as depot battery on the gunnery range at Nowshera.

Here was my first introduction to the totally different view of life of the people inhabiting countries in the East. The range was used to calibrate guns, which necessitated an accurate survey of the intended targets. When the guns fired a safety officer was posted to the target area, as well as on the gun position. This was necessary because the local Pathans had the habit of tying their aged relatives to the targets. If the safety officer did not spot them in time, then the regiment had to pay out – five rupees for a grandfather and three rupees for a grandmother – when they were killed. This was a very different set of social customs from those prevailing in Europe.

*   *   *

The regiment left India after I had been with them for a few months and went by troopship to Singapore, where it arrived in October 1941 and immediately left for Malaya. Training for the different terrain now began, including altering the camouflage on the vehicles and getting used to jungle conditions.

Arriving in Malaya on 10 October, the regiment was billeted near Ipoh, in northern Malaya. On the 1 December our battery was sent to Kelantan, and the other battery of the regiment and the regimental headquarters were sent to Kuantan, both places on the east coast of Malaya. We went by road from Ipoh to Kuala Lumpur, and there entrained for Kelantan, the train journey taking over fifteen hours.

The train arrived at Kuala Krai, at the southern end of the state of Kelantan, and there we alighted. The officers went to the Rest House, one of the government basic buildings for the accommodation of government officers when on tour. It was on a small hill, about 100 feet high, with a restaurant on the first floor. On the wall in the restaurant was a line about six feet high, marking the flood level for 1926, showing the whole state had been under water at that time. As we had arrived at the season for flooding this was unsettling.

The battery drove north to the small village of Chondong and waited for further orders. There was information that a Japanese convoy was off the east coast of Malaya and likely to land at Patani in Thailand, or at a beach in Kelantan. The state has a coast line about 100 miles long, roughly equivalent to the coast from Suffolk to the bottom of Kent. To defend this area was one enhanced Indian brigade of six battalions, a battery of mountain artillery, and our battery of 4.5 howitzers in reserve, a total of 32 guns.

In spite of the length of coastline, there were only two places where a landing would be effective because of the lack of communicating roads. These places were Sabak beach near Kota Bharu, and Kumassin beach, about 50 miles down the coast from Kota Bharu.

At 10.30pm on the 7 December the Japanese started shelling and landing at Sabak beach; 10.30pm in Malaya was the same time as 2.30am on 7 December at Pearl Harbor. Brigadier Keys, in charge of the troops in Kelantan, informed Malay Command of the attack, who, in turn, informed the UK, who informed America – so the attack on Pearl Harbor five hours later should not have come as a surprise.

The battery set off before midnight to a position on the perimeter of the airfield at Kota Bharu, about two miles from the town, and a mile or so from the beach. We set up a gun position in a rubber estate, that being the only suitable position in an area of scrub and pineapple plantations. We could not fire because the Royal Australian Air Force planes were taking off from the airfield to bomb the Japanese convoy – with great success; they sank two transports out of three.

The RAAF evacuated the airfield in mid-afternoon when the Japanese attack made their position untenable; the battery was then able to start firing on enemy positions between the beach and the airfield, in support of the defending Dogra battalion. On the morning of the 9 December the Japanese began to take over the airfield, so the battery withdrew; our last task was to destroy the oil tanks on our side of the airfield. Early that morning we passed through the town of Kota Bharu and took up a position about a mile south of the town.

The Japanese captured Kota Bharu town late in the afternoon and the battery withdrew to the first of three main defensive positions on the road leading from Kota Bharu to Kuala Krai. This position was in the grounds of a bungalow overlooking a small river, and was held for a couple of days until the Japanese infiltrated through the jungle to the back of the position. The brigade then withdrew – with the battery providing support from a series of temporary positions, using two guns at a bend in the road – in a series of leap-frogs between the three main positions.

The battery's next position was at a crossroads with one road leading to Kumassin; one battalion retreated from Kumassin beach down this road to join the rest of the brigade. This position lasted only just over a day. The Japanese infantry could easily filter through the jungle and attack the rear of the positions. They commandeered bicycles from local shops and local people, and used them to cycle swiftly along paths through rubber estates and jungle. The Japanese High Command admitted that a lot of their successful infantry attacks, both on the east and west coasts, depended on the availability of bicycles and good roads and paths for cycling.

There were now insufficient troops available in the brigade to defeat this tactic of outflanking the second main defended position. The brigade therefore withdrew and continued to leap-frog down the road until it reached the last main position, which was defending a padi swamp, with the Japanese having to attack across the padi (cultivated rice plants). The defence lasted longer than was expected because it was difficult for the Japanese to outflank the position.

This last main position defended Kuala Krai, the railhead for Kelantan. South of Kuala Krai was a hundred miles of jungle, with numerous small rivers and swamps, and only the railway made its way through this difficult terrain to Kuala Lipis. It was essential that we held Kuala Krai while trains came from Kuala Lipis to evacuate as much of the brigade as was possible. The infantry were reduced to two battalions, with one troop of our battery supporting the infantry; the other battalions, together with supply units and the other gun troop of our battery, were put on a train. The last train drew in to take the transport, Brigade Headquarters, ammunition, and all but two of the remaining guns. These last two guns kept up a random bombardment for a couple of hours while the train was being loaded, then they were speedily entrained about midnight – a difficult task in the darkness. The train then left, with two battalions marching along the railway track, and the next morning arrived at Kuala Lipis station. It was unloaded and the battery went to a hide in a large rubber estate.

Orders were received to go to Kuala Lumpur, but as Japanese planes were active over Kuala Lipis the move was deferred until nightfall. The night trip was hazardous because the very narrow road wound over the mountains through a pass – the Gap – with hairpin bends. Kuala Lumpur was reached at daybreak and Headquarters contacted. After expressing surprise that no accidents had occurred it ordered the battery to Port Swettenham on the west coast of Malaya, about half way down the peninsular.

Having reached Port Swettenham the battery received orders to guard the coast from Kuala Selangor to Morib, a stretch of about 80 miles, with Port Swettenham roughly in the middle of the coastline. There were three places where a landing could take place with a communicating road system; these were Kuala Selangor, Port Swettenham, and Morib. Two guns were sent to Kuala Selangor, two to Morib, and the remaining four guns kept at Port Swettenham.

A battalion of the Malay Volunteer Force and a battery of guns from the Malay Volunteer Force were sent as reinforcements, so our battery was redeployed with a troop of four guns at each of Kuala Selangor and Morib.

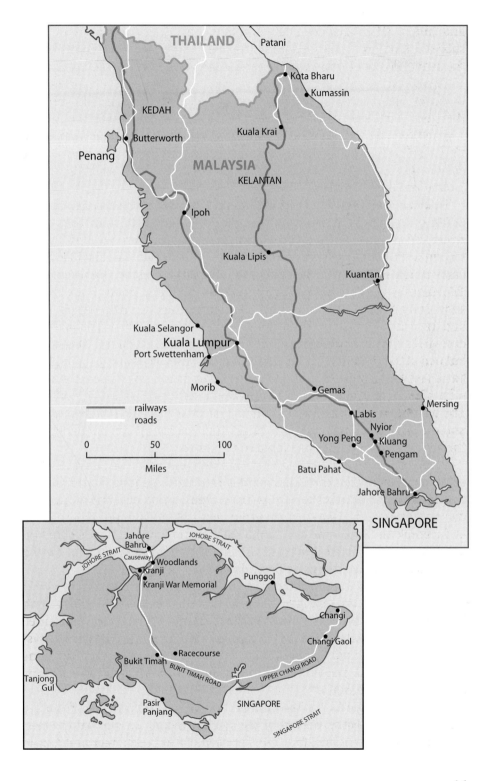

THAILAND

Patani

Kota Bharu

Kumassin

KEDAH

Kuala Krai

Butterworth

Penang

MALAYSIA

KELANTAN

Ipoh

Kuala Lipis

Kuantan

Kuala Selangor

Kuala Lumpur

Port Swettenham

Morib

Gemas

Mersing

Labis

Nyior

Yong Peng

Kluang

Pengam

railways
roads

Batu Pahat

0   50   100

Jahore Bahru

Miles

SINGAPORE

Jahore Bahru

JOHORE STRAIT

JOHORE STRAIT

Causeway

Woodlands

Kranji

Punggol

Kranji War Memorial

Changi

Changi Gaol

Bukit Timah

Racecourse

Tanjong Gul

BUKIT TIMAH ROAD

UPPER CHANGI ROAD

SINGAPORE

Pasir Panjang

SINGAPORE STRAIT

Port Swettenham was defended by the MVF. A fleet of small boats full of Japanese troops attacking Kuala Selangor was repulsed by accurate gun fire with several boats sunk; air raids were experienced in Port Swettenham, but no land attacks.

Kuala Lumpur is about 30 miles from Port Swettenham and an enemy alert was given when the Japanese started to attack it on the 6 January. The town fell on the 11 January, but by that time the battery had withdrawn down the main north-south trunk road. It joined the rest of the regiment at Labis, but we were soon separated. The two batteries were used to support a retreat, again in leap-frog fashion down the trunk road.

At Gemas the railway from the east coast joined the tracks from the west coast, and with the Japanese advancing down both road and railway, the positions on the trunk road could have been attacked from the rear. There a strong defensive position was established, with the regiment in support. We had started the war with the regiment in the 9th Indian Division, defending the east coast. With casualties in the 9th and 11th Indian Divisions the remaining troops were united in the 11th Division, and formed the force at Gemas,

The battery fired many rounds from this position, with one particularly bizarre action. The troop commander in his observation post (OP), underneath a bungalow on stilts, suddenly became aware of Japanese troops sitting round the post watching him. With presence of mind he ordered two rounds of gunfire on the OP. When the shells landed the Japanese ran for shelter, and he and his assistant OP gunner hastily escaped to the battery without being shot at. We were then ordered to retreat because there were now no infantry to provide covering fire for our position.

The whole division retreated down the trunk road to Yong Peng, while the battery was ordered to Rengam. Rengam is at the crossroads where the north-south trunk road is crossed by the road connecting Batu Pahat on the west coast with Mersing on the east coast; the distance between the two towns is about 80 miles. The plan was to establish a front line north of the Mersing road, using the road for communications between defended positions. The battery was ordered to find a position between Rengam and Kluang, a distance of about 20 miles, south of the road, and contact the Australian brigade which had been ordered to defend the road between these towns.

We searched, but could find no Australian troops, so extended our reconnaissance to Kluang, where we found a Sikh battalion, part of a brigade of the Indian army, defending the town. The Indian battalion was overjoyed to have artillery support, so we moved the battery along the road to Kluang. The next day the Sikhs were ordered to Nyior, and we accompanied them.

Nyior is a small village, just north of Kluang, on the railway line from Gemas to Singapore; the Japanese were advancing down the line to cut off

Mersing. Our task was to prevent this manoeuvre by defending Nyior. The Sikhs and the battery advanced up the road from Kluang until the advance guard bumped into the enemy. Hurriedly taking up a position in the labourers' lines of a rubber estate, the battery engaged the Japanese and their advance was halted.

Firing began at 1000 yards, but as the enemy advanced the range dropped until we were firing at 450 yards, which is getting rather close for artillery support. While we were firing at this range the platoon of Sikhs guarding the gun position intimated that the Japanese had infiltrated past the battalion and were attacking us in the rear. We led a bayonet charge from the battery position and drove them off. The Sikh battalion then mounted an attack and the Japanese temporarily retreated again.

The battery commander had been shot while directing gun fire from his OP, and was driven back to brigade headquarters. As the enemy outnumbered us the commanding officer of the Sikhs decided to withdraw. We later discovered that the Sikhs and ourselves had been fighting a full Japanese division.* The battery retreated down the road, but not back to Kluang because that area was under heavy attack; we were advised to aim for Johore Bharu, the town on the Johore Strait, at the Causeway joining Singapore island to the mainland.

During the night the battery made its way through a rubber estate at Layang Layang, getting lost because no maps showed the roads through this very large estate. However, by dawn on the 30 January we arrived at Johore Bharu, and waited there to make contact with any army headquarters we could find. We did finally make contact and were ordered to cross the Causeway, go to the village of Woodlands and await further instructions.

Eventually, orders came through to go to the village of Ponggol on the north coast of the island and to establish a battery position there. Arriving at Punggol we found a zoo, surrounded by marshy land. It was pointed out to headquarters that no gun position was feasible, so off we were sent to the Tampinis road near Changi, still on the north coast of the island facing the Johore Straits. We still could find no infantry to support; reinforcements were expected, but were not yet in position.

Further orders then moved us to Tanjong Gul, a headland on the southwest corner of Singapore island. There we found the 44th Indian Brigade; they had not formed a defensive position, so we did not prepare a gun position. Instead we formed a hide in a rubber estate, and waited for further information. When reconnoitring possible OPs and gun positions on the 5 January I saw the convoy of reinforcements being heavily bombed while making its way to Singapore harbour.

* Information from *Japan's Greatest Victory, Britain's Worst Defeat*, by Colonel Masanobu Tsuji, a senior Japanese staff officer.

On 6 January the battery itself was subjected to pattern bombing by the Japanese, with the bombs washing over the hide, like sea breaking over a beach. We had several casualties – lessened by effective slit trenches – but lost no guns or ammunition. There was still no information concerning enemy activity, or orders to prepare positions for defence. On the night of the 8 February the Japanese attacked, landing in a marshy area near Kranji, a village on the north-west of Singapore island, north of our position.

The area around Kranji was defended by the Australians, and we heard the news of the landing on the Singapore radio on the morning of 9 February, but still received no orders. Listening to further Singapore news broadcasts, we heard that the Japanese had advanced to Bukit Timah village. To get back to Singapore town the battery had to go through Bukit Timah, and we now had no radio contact with all other formations.

It was decided that we would retreat to Bukit Timah between 9pm and 2am; the Japanese usually began operations at 4.30am every day. Driving at 5mph to reduce the noise of the vehicles, the battery inched its way along the road. The convoy drove through any Japanese positions – and also the positions of the British troops around Bukit Timah – and arrived safely about 3am, to everyone's surprise.

We dug in gun positions east of Bukit Timah and looked for infantry to support; on finding infantry the battery fired a few rounds. The Japanese, as usual, succeeded in outflanking the position, and we were ordered to retreat to Buona Vista road to safeguard a river position, but on arrival we were instructed to retreat to Holland Road. Having found a suitable position, east of Holland Road, the area was reconnoitred and we came upon some armoured cars guarding a cross-road. They were about to retreat and the officer in charge advised us to get into Singapore city.

The battery hastily reformed on the road and drove towards Singapore, through Japanese troops taking up positions on one side of the road and British troops on the other. Luck held, and the battery, going about 50mph, escaped with only a few bullet holes through the trucks. Continuing on, the battery arrived at the sea front and took up a position on Beach Road, with the gun trails in the monsoon drain at the side of the road. A command post was established in Raffles Hotel, obliquely in front of the guns.

The British forces formed a perimeter around Singapore city in the shape of a semicircle, with both ends at the sea front. A battalion of the Malay Regiment defended a position at Pasir Panjang, a strip of land on the western end of the perimeter. This position had its back to the sea and stuck out of the perimeter like a long finger. In the afternoon the acting battery commander found the Malay battalion and offered support, which was gratefully accepted. The date was the 12 February and it was late afternoon when the battery became heavily engaged with prolonged firing. In spite of repeated attacks the Malay battalion held firm and refused to withdraw from its position.

Friday, the 13 February, was a day of constant attacks, accompanied by heavy bombing and shelling. Water was running short in Singapore city as the reservoirs and the pipe line from Johore had been captured. By the morning of the 15 February, Lieutenant-General Percival, the Commander-in-Chief of the Malayan Forces, had decided that further resistance was not possible, and negotiations for surrender were started.

The command was received by the battery that hostilities would cease at 4pm on the 15th, and at 3pm the last order was given for 43 rounds of gun-fire on Racecourse Village. The ammunition was now completely expended so the gunners removed the nuts on the recoil mechanism of the guns; if the guns were fired they could explode. This task was completed just before the ceasefire.

The battery joined the rest of the regiment and settled down for the night of the 15 February on the sea side of the Padang, the open space at the centre of Singapore. On the morning of the 16 February the guns and vehicles were parked in a field near Tanglin, and the battery marched off to captivity at Changi, carrying whatever belongings we could manage on a twenty-mile walk.

The long march to Changi ended the first night at a small village, called Tanah Merah, where RAF personnel had been billeted. We went thankfully into the empty huts, with a lot of overcrowding, and settled down to sleep. The next day some food was organized and we looked at our surroundings – a village near the sea shore on the eastern side of Singapore island, about a mile short of Changi. The day passed uneventfully, checking on all ranks to see whether the stragglers had arrived safely.

The next night was interrupted by some rifle fire and other explosions, making us wonder whether the capitulation had been completed. In the morning, after a meal, we explored the sea shore, not seeing any Japanese in the vicinity. At the other end of a shallow bay, we saw a 'bunch' of Chinese, roped together, all dead. The bodies looked like a bundle of fire-wood, and appeared to have been machine-gunned while roped together. The corpses were lying against each other, some just off the ground, but most of them slumped down, some almost on their knees.

The Japanese hated – and feared – the Chinese, so had apparently lost no time in rounding up all those they suspected of being able to make some form of resistance. It was puzzling as to why these Chinese had been roped together before execution, but we presumed it was the quickest method of dealing with a mass execution. As we thought we could see Japanese soldiers near the dead Chinese, we decided a closer inspection was unwise.

With hands bound, and roped together, the Chinese would have been unable to escape the rounds from a machine gun; they could not run away, as they all faced in different directions. Those in the centre of the bunch were immobilized by those at the edge who had been killed first. One could imagine the thoughts of those in the centre of the group, when those on the outside were being shot, while they on the inside could do nothing to evade the bullets. As far as we could see from a distance, none was left alive. The tide was rising and lapping over the feet of those nearest the sea.

Shortly after this unpleasant experience the regiment was paraded and on its way to Changi, where we were imprisoned in Changi Gaol. The sight of the execution had raised doubts about our own fate; we could only guess at the reasons for the execution of the Chinese and feared the Japanese might deal with us in the same manner. As it turned out this was not the case, only POWs attempting to escape were in danger of execution when caught.

Interlude

THE DESCRIPTION OF THE CAMPAIGN in Malaya, and of my previous experiences, can be viewed through Western thought which has a set of rules for conduct, for both peace time and war time. Both British and Indian soldiers followed these rules. The ensuing description of life under the Japanese has to be viewed through Eastern thought, as explained below.

Whenever POW and Japanese are associated in British minds, the words 'torture' and 'brutality' are recalled by the majority of people. Torture implies the infliction of intense pain for revenge, cruelty, or to extract information; only the latter is really applicable to POWs, since the Japanese adhered to the POW conventions of the 1907 agreement. The Japanese had no need to interrogate POWs on military information, as it was no longer relevant. Escape was a subject for interrogation for the very few who attempted it, as the nearest friendly territory was either 2000 miles north of Thailand, or 3000 miles south, and none succeeded in reaching safety. Clandestine radio sets, and broadcast information, were the main object of POW interrogation, and members of signal units were prime subjects for questioning. For most POWs, however, interrogation was rarely seen, or heard of.

Brutality is subject to a wide interpretation, both historically and globally. In Britain, views on brutality have changed over the years; it is only just over 120 years ago that flogging in the British army was abolished, and Queen Victoria wondered how discipline could be maintained, as it was then considered a normal punishment. The Korean and Taiwanese guards were mainly responsible for any brutality suffered by POWs on the Burma-Siam railway, but the ill-treatment of Asian coolies working on the railway was far worse and has rarely been mentioned. The majority of British prisoners in Thailand came from 18 Division, whose troops had no experience of Eastern thought and customs, so judged their treatment by Western standards. This is probably the reason why brutality has been the subject of much sensationalism.

No Japanese soldier considered surrendering, as if he did, he could no longer return to his town or village and maintain his honour. The number of Japanese taken prisoner was very small and, in 1945, many Japanese soldiers were doubtful about surrendering, even though the Emperor had commanded it. This coloured the Japanese view of British POWs, considering such soldiers beneath contempt. The Japanese also held the Indian National Army (INA) in contempt as turncoats, and still hold the Koreans and

THE MARCH TO TARSAO. *Part of the journey was through jungle, along a muddy track which had been churned up by lorries. Prisoners and guards were wearied and stretched out over quite a distance. All semblance of an organised march had disappeared.*

after them. While we were happy to be resting there, the place itself filled us with gloom.

We were now in monsoon tropical jungle and though it was not as thick as tropical rain forest jungle, the tall trees gave it an eerie appearance. Lianas hung from the trees and the sunlight was greatly reduced in the shade – it was not unlike a dim cathedral.

After our two-day respite we fell in and were marched off at dawn, following a dirt road which climbed steadily uphill away from Tarsao. We were now entering the foothills which led to the mountainous interior region of Thailand. Almost immediately troops began to straggle but were shepherded along by the guards with shouts of '*Kura kura bugero*', which roughly translated means 'get a move on, you lazy so and so'. Slow walkers were encouraged with a rifle butt as speed seemed to be required. Later we saw the reason for this speed.

We marched for about six kilometres and then suddenly in the middle of nowhere on the dirt road through the jungle, the guards said 'Camp'. We asked 'Where'. The answer was 'Here'.

We were nonplussed, but lorries arrived carrying tools and kitchen equipment, so we realized we had to make a camp in the jungle there and then. Hence the speed; the guards also wanted a camp made for them before night fell.

The lorries delivered machetes, *changkols*, Assam forks, and root extractors. *Changkols* are spades attached at right angles to a haft; Assam forks are forks similarly attached at right angles to a haft. The British army in the First World War used an entrenching tool which was shaped like a *changkol*. They are excellent tools for digging up earth and were always in use on the railway.

The battalion was organized into parties to fell the trees, bamboos and other growth, to move the felled wood, remove the tree stumps, and flatten the earth. The first space cleared was for the cookhouse so that a midday meal could be provided; after that a general space was cleared to form the camp area.

All ranks took part in the clearing operation and a space rapidly appeared in the jungle. We were higher than the coastal plain, the jungle was much less dense and mainly characterized by a lot of bamboo.

Bamboo grows in clumps with different varieties having different girths and different heights. All had shoots growing at the base of the clump and these took a lot of excavation to get the ground clear. There are male and female bamboos, with the female having a hollow stem and the male having a solid stem; the diameter of a male stem is less than that of a female stem. In the clump female bamboos vastly outnumbered male bamboos.

Bamboos flower very rarely – only once in every thirty to forty years –

CAMP IN THE JUNGLE. *Monsoon tropical jungle is not as thick as tropical rain forest jungle, but it took us three days to clear enough space for a tented camp. The tall trees gave it an eerie appearance; lianas hung from the trees and the sunlight was greatly reduced in the shade – it was not unlike a dim cathedral.*

and when they do the whole vegetation dies and a new generation grows up in place of the former generation. Such facts took time to find out, but we gradually learnt as we came to use bamboo more and more in all our work.

As we cleared the ground, tree trunks, branches and tall bamboos fell against us; the work force was closely packed to achieve maximum clearance. We did not know then how dangerous growing bamboo was. Only later did we learn that a cut caused by a bamboo stem almost always turned into a trophical ulcer.

I was working next to a member of the Volunteer force and as we were cutting down a large clump of bamboo a tall stem fell across our legs. We took no notice of it and went on working.

That night I bathed my leg as it felt itchy, but I think my co-worker did not. I developed a scratch which was red, but after bathing it every night it vanished to leave three white scars which I had for the rest of my time in Thailand. The Volunteer developed an ulcer and was eventually shipped off to a base camp for sick people. There he lost his leg; it had to be amputated because the ulcer would not heal.

After working all day cutting down the jungle, sufficient space was cleared to erect tents that had been supplied by the Japanese and, having had a meal, we lay down glad of a rest. The next morning we were up before sunrise, fed, and started work again enlarging the clearing. This went on for about three days, by which time we had enough space for a tented camp for the POWs and a separate space for the guards.

The officers were provided with a square Indian Army bell tent, as usual without the outside cover. In this tent twenty officers and their baggage were crammed; some had a fair amount of baggage, but most did not have much. The colonel and the adjutant of the battalion had a separate tent, while the other ranks were crowded into Indian Army tents – either a tent or its cover.

No bedding was supplied, so we lay on the ground, using what material we had against the damp. I had an old gas cape which served as a ground sheet, and I used my pack as a pillow. After eating our food we retired to bed too tired to do anything else, wearing our everyday clothes as we had nothing to change into. Food was eaten squatting on our belongings.

On about the third or fourth night we were lying on our piece of ground, and I was trying to get to sleep but finding it difficult. Suddenly I heard a quiet, querulous whisper from one of the occupants lying two officers away from me. He said 'Is anyone awake?' The following conversation then took place in whispers, with me answering the plaintive call. 'Yes Jones I am awake, what's the matter?' 'There's a snake up my trouser leg.' 'Where is the snake's head?' 'Too bloody close.' 'OK, I'll wake the rest quietly and we'll see what we can do.'

Luckily the *gunso* had a good sense of humour, so we both laughed off that episode – but it could have been a nasty encounter.

Little by little the *gunso's* background came to light in our general conversations. He was a regular soldier and had fought in China before being sent to Java, but had not fought in Malaya. He had a wife and two children in Japan, and complained he had not seen his wife for seven years. Maybe it had only seemed like seven years as, presumably, he had passed through Japan on his way to Java from China.

I had the feeling that he wanted to talk with us rather than with the guards, because he considered us front-line soldiers and the guards just POW watchers. It is true we had committed the unforgivable sin of surrendering, but he appreciated we had been ordered to surrender rather than doing it on our own volition.

It was with Oburi that we had discussed the disciplinary methods of the Japanese army, as described previously. Oburi was a good disciplinarian, and kept the guards well under control. Face slapping was reduced to a complete minimum and towards the end of our stay in Tonchan South, practically vanished.

Oburi gradually became friendly towards the officers, and visited us frequently in our tent. One of the reasons for describing him in some detail, was that his life and mine were curiously entwined; later, he saved my life.

*   *   *

While I was still convalescing I started my new jobs of interpreter and trader with the barges. Because the battalion had lost so many troops from the cholera epidemic, reinforcements appeared. These included Dutch, British, Australian, and even a few Americans who had been captured from naval vessels fighting in the Dutch East Indies. One of these Americans was a naval officer who came to live in our tent, and from him we learned of the battles in the Coral Sea, and the odds against which they had had to fight.

The working parties were now facing even more difficult conditions. Working in the rain was unpleasant and caused more sickness. The earth was that much heavier to dig and carry and the work under construction could be washed away by the rain.

One night there was an exceptionally heavy storm and the whole camp was woken by the guards well before the normal time of roll call. The command was 'oru men and oru elephanto' ('all men and all elephants'). All the men who were not desperately ill in the hospital were paraded and marched off to a gulley some distance from the camp.

The heavy rain had washed away some of the soil and all the uprights for the bridge across the gulley had collapsed like a pack of cards and were lying one on top of the other. We thought this was going to be a very lengthy operation, but no, the engineers had a solution. Ropes were tied around the uprights and all the men and all the elephants pulled as hard as they could. Very slowly, all the timbers came upright into their correct position, and were as they had been erected. The engineers then hurriedly produced some rails and laid them across the horizontal beams of the uprights. An engineer then went across on each side of the bridge and hammered in nails to fix the rails to the horizontal beams. When the engineers had finished they had a bridge with a set of rails across it but we hoped we would never be on a train crossing that particular bridge.

The work of repairing the bridge was finished by the end of the morning and we returned to camp for a belated breakfast. In the afternoon the working parties went out again on their normal tasks.

At that stage of the railway construction the repaired bridge was adequate; there was little traffic on the line as yet. The Japanese had adapted lorries to travel on the rails by removing the road wheels and replacing them with flanged railway wheels. These lorries were light enough to go over the repaired bridge without doing any damage. Occasionally, a lorry would tow a couple of railway wagons and this, too, did not affect the bridge.

Besides the work on the railway there was another unpleasant task, which was the burying of the dead. We had considerable numbers in the camp who needed to be buried, and the Japanese did not want to spare too many men on this task as the railway had precedence.

We would have preferred to burn the corpses, but it was hard enough trying to get enough dry wood for the cooking fires and the fires to provide boiled water for the hospital. The wood was damp from the rains and in any case cremation would have to take place in the open, with the very likely occurrence of rain to make it impossible.

The solution was communal graves. A large pit was dug and the dead thrown in. Individual graves were not allowed because that would mean clearing more jungle to make space for the graves. The pits were gradually filled with the dead and earth piled on top; presumably the adjutant kept records of who was buried and where.

Not only did we have to cope with our own dead but one day we were detailed as a burial party to go to a labourers' camp. It was impossible to count the number of dead, as they were lying everywhere. All of the deaths were from cholera, and it looked as if more than half the camp had died. We estimated at least two hundred dead, and having dug a pit, the bodies were thrown into it. When all had gone in we shovelled earth on top. By now it was getting dusk but just as we thought we had finished we saw the odd hand still sticking up through the earth. More earth was thrown on top and padded down. Only then could men and guards return wearily back to camp.

In between going on these burial parties I went down to the river to meet the Thai trading barges. Standing by the bank I could see that the river was still swollen with the heavy rains. In addition to the trees that were floating down the stream, there were now bodies, presumably of cholera victims; the water from the river was definitely unsafe for any purpose unless it had been thoroughly boiled.

Apart from cholera the troops still suffered from the original complaints. Malaria had become worse as the mosquitoes had increased with the rains. Trophical ulcers had also increased as the wet conditions hastened the onset of sores and other skin diseases.

One of the skin diseases now appearing was scabies, caused no doubt by the lack of washing facilities. I found that I had this intensely irritating disease and went to see the doctor. He had nothing to cure it, but suggested some treatment.

The Japanese had organized a supply of electricity by wires stretched along wooden poles running by the side of the road. The voltage was high and the conducting wires were mounted on porcelain insulators; inside the insulators were blocks of sulphur.

Sulphur was the required cure for scabies. At night we crept out of the camp, past the guards, and shinned up the electricity poles. Takinggreat care, we lifted the porcelain insulators and took out the block of sulphur. We then returned quietly to the camp.

The next step was to purchase some red palm oil or coconut oil. The sulphur was then scraped thinly and put into the oil. When the preparation was complete, the next thing was to borrow an old petrol can to boil some water.

Everything was now ready for the cure. With the aid of a friend you stripped off all your clothes, which were put into the boiling water and continued to be boiled. This did not improve the clothes but was essential to get rid of the scabies mites.

The last piece of equipment was a nail brush and some soap. The skin was now scrubbed with the brush and soap until all the scabies pustules bled. This was not too bad on the back but the belly was more painful and on the scrotum was excruciatingly painful. After scrubbing, the mixture of sulphur and oil was applied to the whole skin. The application produced great irritation, and naked men could be seen jumping up and down, swearing like troopers, as the sulphur got to work. When the irritation had died down, and the clothes had dried, you could dress again, ready for the next round.

This treatment had to be repeated for three days running, after which you could assume you had conquered the scabies mite. Care had to be taken not to become reinfected. I managed the treatment and, fortunately, did not have a recurrence in that camp. The main object of eliminating scabies was to avoid the complication of sceptic scabies which was more difficult to treat. The *gunso* connived at men leaving the camp to get the sulphur and the guards did not stop them. He probably realized that curing the disease was essential to keeping the troops working; this was another example of his enlightened control of the camp.

I had one more bout of skin disease. At night I started to itch at the base of my stomach. No amount of scratching seemed to alleviate the itch, so off to the doctor once more. I described the complaint and he said 'Lower your shorts and I'll have a look at it'. I did so and he burst out laughing and said 'You've got crabs – pubic lice to the uninformed – and there's not a woman within fifty miles of the camp. After this I'll believe in the lavatory seat theory of the propagation of venereal diseases.'

I said that was all very well but what was he going to do about my crabs. 'Simple' said he, 'fetch me your razor'. And with that he shaved off all the pubic hairs. A thorough wash with some boiled water and soap, and once again I could face the world without itching.

Shortly after this incident the Japanese decided to do something about our health and produced smallpox vaccine. We were all duly vaccinated, although there never had been any sign of smallpox. It was just a gesture by the Japanese Higher Command to show they were taking care of us.

Now that the news of the cholera epidemic had percolated through to Japanese headquarters, it was decided that POWs should be tested for the disease. Japanese doctors appeared and proceeded to give the glass rod test* to all personnel. We were accustomed to this treatment, but after a while the Japanese ran out of glass rods so improvised with bamboo sticks. This test was most unpleasant, particularly if the bamboo had any splinters on it. The results of these tests never became known, so probably it was just another public relations effort.

The Japanese in the camp had realized the necessity for boiling water. They brought fifty gallon oil drums to their hutted camp, and used them for boiling water. The drums were filled with water, the POWs supplied wood for the fire, and the Japanese enjoyed hot baths every day. We were duly envious.

By strict adherence to the hygiene rules the incidence of cholera now fell. The troops continued on working parties, but the insistence on speed was reduced and the work became slightly easier. The railway had advanced nearer to Tonchan and the trains provided a better supply of food.

This gave the officers less work to do and more time was spent in our tents. When work was slack the hours were spent in conversation, there being no alternative for passing the time. Discussion seemed to be led by the Catholic padre, and the other officers joined in.

---

* As explained in Chapter III this involves thrusting the glass rod up the anus, giving it a twirl to remove some faeces, then making a faeces smear on a glass dish.

Naturally enough with the padre a common topic was religion. The arguments were lengthy because both officers and men had developed an antipathy to the efforts of the priests in camp. The officers tended to agree with the troop's description of padres as 'God botherers'. Perhaps it was not entirely the padres' fault, as there was not much spiritual comfort they could give to the troops, considering the conditions under which we all lived.

The padre insisted that if we had faith we would survive, implying that it was his particular brand of faith. Two of us, the doctor and I, said in that case the survival rate should be higher amongst Catholics than other believers or non-believers, whereas the statistics of death did not support the belief in his faith.

On looking at the men who died there was no apparent pattern, and disease and death were indiscriminate in their incidence. We had one or two officers who had worked in the East for some time and they proffered their knowledge of other religions in that region. None of the religions seemed to offer any explanation of why some died and some lived; it did not appear to depend on their actions or their beliefs. All afflictions had a random distribution, although individual actions could have a bearing on the incidence.

The Buddhist religion states that all men are responsible for their own actions and that was accepted by us as the nearest approach to an answer for the present situation. We were not so sure about the second tenet of Buddhism, that merit or sin determined the future existence in the next incarnation, that *karma* was immortal.

The doctor and I were determined defenders of the concept of random action as this fitted in with the scientific concept of the laws of chaos. If nature could not distinguish between any two electrons at one and the same time, then there would appear to be a parallel case that the recording of the specific actions of any one person should also be in doubt.

Although this argument appealed to us, we acknowledged that religion could provide some comfort to people who did not want to argue for an impersonal approach to the incidents of life. These discussions provided a means of passing the time but never led to any justifiable conclusions. We were now waiting to go on to the next stage of our training as railway builders.

CHAPTER VII

I'm dreaming of a white Christmas

ORDERS CAME THROUGH that the battalion was to be despatched to camps higher up the river. Those considered not fit to march would stay behind, and about one hundred and fifty remained in the camp. We had had so many changes with reinforcements to replace sick personnel that the remainder were a very mixed collection and it was difficult to recognize the original battalion.

After the contingent to go up country had marched out the remainder reorganized the accommodation, giving all of us much more space in the tents. Small working parties were detailed for camp fatigues and, as the health of the POWs improved, outside working parties were once again organized.

The Japanese had been hurrying the construction of the railway again and the track now reached the camp. There was a special force for the actual laying of the track and members of this force passed through our area.

We spoke to the members of the force and realized they were receiving better treatment in the way of food and tented accommodation than we were. We put this down to the force being specially recruited for a specialist job. They also had a detachment of medical staff with them. A party, called K Force, had been assembled to provide medical care for the POW camps in Thailand. This K Force had been split into detachments to accompany the different groups of POWs who had come to Thailand before us.

The track was laid on the earth of the embankments that we had built and also across the bridges that we had constructed. There were passing points made with double tracks; the majority of the line was single track. Presumably there was a method of signalling but we were not aware of it. Telephone communication was apparent as we could receive orders from other areas.

The working parties now being sent out had much lighter work than the work previously allotted to the camp. The embankments, ridges and cuttings were all finished and the task of our parties was just tidying up the track area.

Trains driven by the converted lorries brought material and rations to the camp; the material included ballast. The POWs were issued with pickaxes and they had to lever up the sleepers of the track and put ballast underneath them. At the same time the working party had to lay ballast between the sleepers and level it off; the result was a finished railway, complete with sleepers, rails and ballast. This work was light enough for the troops to recover their health and the number of fit men increased as time went on.

The parties were organized under officers as before; there were six or seven left in the camp besides the Anglican padre, one doctor, and the accountant. The Roman Catholic padre and the other two doctors had accompanied the troops sent up country

Both the padre and the accountant travelled up the road to other camps, the padre conducting services and the accountant keeping track of the men's wages and producing pay for all of us. As officers we drew our thirty yen a month – the deductions for accommodation, food and paper still being made although nothing was supplied.

Japanese troops were now beginning to use the road, so presumably the way from Thailand to Burma must have been clear. Almost every day a detachment of troops would pass the camp, hauling equipment on two-wheeled, light carts with ropes attached to the carts. These were piled high with sacks and boxes, but it was difficult to see what were the contents. Although the rains had abated the road was muddy and the troop movements made the surface worse.

Many times the carts would get bogged down in the mud and more men were needed to extricate them. This was accompanied by much shouting, with officers and NCOs yelling at the men for a greater effort. There was obviously a need for speed.

Light artillery was also hauled along the road, including ammunition in carts. All of it was shifted by man power; no draught animals were used. The soldiers were armed and, from their appearance, bound for the front in Burma. They had a very long way to go, over three hundred miles to the southern part of Burma, so it seemed a strange way to transport troops.

The railway was not usable for heavy traffic, as yet, so marching on foot was the only method of transferring the soldiers from Thailand. The sight of these troop movements cheered us up – if the Japanese army was reduced to moving troops in this fashion, then the war could not be going so well for them. We were also cheered by the sight of Japanese troops being shouted at, in the same way as we were shouted at by our guards.

The travels of the padre and accountant to the other camps allowed them to bring back news of the outside world. We learnt that Italy had been invaded and the war was now going well for the Allies. The end of the war seemed a long way off – but at least the news was no longer so discouraging and we had hopes of one day ending our POW existence. Nobody expected to be home by this Christmas, but we thought there was a possibility of the next Christmas. We had no radio in the camp so we were entirely dependent on the padre and the accountant for any news.

The padre, unfortunately, did not have a good memory. I think his experiences had unnerved him to some extent as he was always a very quiet person. To help his memory he used to write down the news on a small piece of paper and hide it under the elastic band that kept up his stockings. He was better clothed than the rest of us because he had not undertaken any physical work or the organization of outside working parties.

Normally the Japanese never interfered with the priests of any denomination, but one day the padre was searched and the paper hidden in his stockings came to light. He did not reappear at the camp for some time and when he did he was quieter than ever. Apparently the Japanese soldiers had obtained from him the source of his news.

This started a thorough searching of all camps and of all accommodation and personnel in the camps. More than one radio was discovered and the Japanese became very angry. The radio operators were caught and paraded round the camps. At our camp in Tonchon South, a Japanese officer, who was the senior interpreter, came to give the officers a lecture which was to be passed on to the troops. He worked himself into a fury about the discovery of the radios, beginning quietly enough emphasising how wicked it was to secrete radios to hear the false propaganda from the Western allies. The Japanese were looking after us so well – with all the usual comments on the fact that POWs were not worthy of such treatment.

As the lecture proceeded his voice rose and he said 'You British think we Japanese bloody fools. You think we do not know what you do. You think we do not know that you are hiding radios. You think we know f*** nothing but really we know f*** all'. This no doubt was to show off his command of the English idiom; we dare not laugh as that would have been extremely foolish – and dangerous.

From his accent, the Japanese officer must have learnt his English in America, which may have explained why he was not conversant with true English idiom. Of all the Japanese with whom we came into contact, his command of English was probably the best.

The Imperial Japanese Army depended on British and other European interpreters for almost all of their communication with the POWs. The majority of the interpreters had been missionaries, or associated with missions, in Japan. Few British people had learnt Japanese at that time.

However, the troops did laugh when we passed on the message, and we enjoyed a chuckle ourselves. But the incident was not without its tragedy; the radio operators were taken away and once again we never knew what happened to them.

The railway traffic was now beginning to increase and the converted lorries on the system were joined by steam locomotives. These were small engines and where they came from was unknown; they were not like either the Malayan or the Thai locomotives, but much smaller.

This smallness was just as well, because one day, amid great excitement, the Japanese shouted out once again 'Oru men, oru elephanto'. When we arrived at the scene of the request, we were not happy to see a locomotive that had failed to cross a bridge over a gulley. This was the repaired bridge we had worked on before, when it had collapsed with the heavy rain.

When the locomotive had attempted to cross the bridge, the railway lines had bulged outwards and it had slipped down between the rails. Once again we thought this was going to be an impossible task, but no, the engineers solved it. All the men and all the elephants were used to lift the locomotive, and the lines were hurriedly hammered back into shape. Extra sleepers were produced and placed underneath the rails. The lines were quickly nailed to these sleepers and there was the locomotive once more sitting on the rails. For improvisation we could not fault the Japanese engineers.

All bridges in the area were then strengthened in the same way. We wondered whether similar incidents had happened further up the line because there were many such bridges over gulleys, not to mention viaducts over more difficult terrain.

The incidence of disease had dropped because everyone now knew much more about tropical conditions. Bamboo was avoided as far as possible as we knew that contact with it caused ulcers. Trophical ulcers were becoming rarer; all those suffering from them had been despatched to base camps down the river for hospital treatment. Malaria had also declined as the weather was drier and mosquitoes were fewer. We were left with enteric diseases, and dysentery was the chief complaint.

I was no exception and contracted dysentery – diagnosed as amoebic dysentery – and was duly admitted to hospital. I was put into a small tent which was equipped with a *chang* which I lay on. Treatment was still the little black charcoal pills, but we did have a limited supply of M & B 693, which helped.

During the day the camp was almost deserted, with everybody out at work, and I rested on the *chang*, trying to overcome the dysentery. One morning, as I lay in the tent, an elephant's trunk appeared and the sensitive tip passed up and down over my body. It was shortly joined by another trunk. I lay there mesmerized, wondering whether these were wild elephants investigating the tent. It was probable that they were wild because the domesticated elephants had either moved on to another camp or were at work. What would they do?, I was obviously an object of interest to them. They continued, probably for only a few minutes, to investigate me, but it seemed like a lifetime. Eventually they moved off, and I was left alone.

Nobody else in the camp had seen the elephants and some of the orderlies thought that I had dreamt up the whole incident. I assured them I had not – I can still see those trunks waving over me, up and down my body, deciding whether I was friend or foe.

After this frightening encounter, when I went down to the Thai barges to trade, I watched the elephants with more interest. Their drivers would bring them down to the river's edge, remove the shackles from their feet, and let them go into the river. They waded out until the water reached their bellies, then they started to squirt water over themselves. When they had finished their bath they came out of the river of their own accord and waited on the bank while their drivers replaced the shackles, then driver and elephant moved off to their camp. The shackles were iron chains, fixed round their legs just above their feet, with one shackle on each leg. The elephants were hobbled by joining the shackles with a chain.

There were several rafts anchored near the river bank with Thai families living on them. This was the place where the trading barges used to tie up. The rafts were made of bamboo and were quite large, about twenty feet wide by fifty feet long.

A hut, also made of bamboo, was built on each raft with a thatched roof of palm leaves, similar to the *atap* roofs in Malaya. The hut was placed in the middle, so that there was quite a large space all around, with more space at the ends than at the sides. The whole family of the owner lived on the raft, and the children could be seen running about. Strangely, none of the children ever fell in the river.

The rafts were tethered to the bank at both ends and, as the river rose or fell, they either moved out into the river or came closer to the bank. In either case, the position of each raft had to be altered to suit the circumstances. If it were too far out, the current imposed too strong a pull on the tethering ropes. If it were too near, it could run aground on the river bank and upset.

The raft dwellers obtained the help of the elephant drivers, and it was very interesting to see them at work. The driver by some means gave a command to the elephant to move the raft, and the elephant instinctively knew whether to push it in or push it out.

It would wade into the river and if it was pushing the raft in towards the bank, the elephant would put its head against the raft and push in the upstream end first. If it had pushed in the downstream end the raft would have been swept out into the river by the current. The elephant received no guidance and appeared to use its own intelligence.

On completing the task of moving the raft the elephant would have a bath, then come out and wait for its shackles to be put back on its legs. I always watched this performance with admiration.

We had just the one doctor in the camp and the Japanese were now supplying some more drugs, including the M&B 693; the presence of these drugs caused some trouble.

The Japanese army supplied brothels and comfort girls for their troops and the troops were supposed to use them, incurring disciplinary action if they did not. The girls were regularly medically inspected and trouble ensued if they became infected. A Japanese soldier suffering from venereal disease was severely disciplined – even executed if the circumstances warranted it.

Our Korean guards had been replaced by Japanese and one of these new guards, on his leave in a rest camp, had contracted gonorrhoea by not using the official brothels. He came to the medical officer and intimated he wanted some M&B 693 to cure himself. He was told he could not have any of the drug as the supply was not sufficient for the needs of the camp.

The argument between the doctor and the guard continued for two or three days, by which time the guard was becoming frantic. He threatened the doctor, who in the end had to give in and supply him with some tablets of M&B 693. Now came the interesting bit; the supply of the pills given to the guard was enough to stop his symptoms but for a cure he needed a full course of the medicine, which the doctor did not supply.

The guard was christened 'the Nip with the drip', and we wondered what would happen when his symptoms returned. There was some respite because the symptoms were suppressed for several days. Then fortune smiled on us and the guard, with some of his companions, was transferred to another camp. Once again a story with an unknown ending, but we were getting used to not knowing the outcome of many incidents.

I was continuing to act as interpreter for the camp, and translating the orders of the few remaining engineers, via the *gunso*, to the working parties. Periodically the *gunso* would go down to the base camps by train to enjoy a few comfort girls. He must have had a good time because whenever he returned he was very sleepy for two or three days.

During this time the other officers and I became quite friendly with the *gunso* and one day he told me he would like to learn to play bridge. I gathered that the ability to play bridge and golf advanced one's social status considerably in Japan. So here the *gunso* had an admirable opportunity to learn bridge.

I started by teaching him the rudiments of the game in Malay. Then we taught him the numbers in English and also the names of the suits. But trying to get him to understand the aim of the game was laborious, although we succeeded in the end.

Our efforts had other rewards as well, such as a lamp to provide the necessary illumination to play. When he was pleased with his play – and hence grateful – he would produce a tin of condensed milk as a 'presento' to the tent. A tin of condensed milk does not sound much of a gift, but to us it was sheer luxury.

The instruction caused me some amusement, because attempting to translate some words of advice into Malay produced queer results. For instance the following piece of advice sounds quite peculiar in Malay:

89

never take jump take-outs in long suits; many suits have been ruined and rubbers lost in this way. This evoked the question from the *gunso* 'Do I have to jump off my chair?' So I knew that particular piece of advice had not achieved its aim. In the end I gave up trying to provide such pearls of wisdom in Malay.

Most of the soldiers were now working either on outside parties or on fatigues in the camp.. This provided them with money to buy food to supplement their rations, and tobacco. We received no cigarette issue in Thailand, unlike in Malaya, so the purchase of tobacco was a necessity.

The health of all the men was improving and when the working parties set off to the railway line the troops used to sing; popular songs were '*Colonel Bogey*' and '*Bless them all*'.

Due to the easier conditions, better food, and most of them being paid, the troops were also in good spirits. This improvement in outlook appeared to help recovery from illness and the doctor and the rest of us discussed what factors contributed to a person keeping fit under the camp conditions.

I had had a friend in the camp who was a gunner in 18th Division, the force that had arrived in Singapore just in time to be captured. The last contingent arrived only ten days or so before the capitulation. My friend had been a lawyer in a large practice in England and had married the daughter of the head of the firm. He obviously had a bright future before him when he returned to England.

In Singapore and in Thailand he had been the life and soul of the party, always in a good humour and helping his friends when needed. One day he contracted malaria but did not appear to be seriously ill, so probably was suffering from BT malaria, the milder form of the disease. After only seven days, he turned his face to the tent wall and died for no apparent reason.

Perhaps he felt the situation was hopeless and saw no end to his captivity. It could only have been a frame of mind that caused the fatal reaction to the malaria. We had all heard that people in other civilizations could will themselves to die, but we never expected a person from a Western civilization to do just that.

Looking at the men who had survived and those who had died, we decided that one thing of paramount importance was an extended education. The English education system was founded on the idea that '*mens sana in corpore sano*' – a sound mind in a sound body, where the sound body was needed to have the sound mind. Here, under POW circumstances, it appeared that a sound mind was useful in maintaining a sound body, rather than the reverse.

How was a sound mind to be achieved? The mind needed exercise just as the body needs exercise to keep it functioning at its full potential. The only form of mental exercise lay in conversation, because there were no other forms of mental activity available with our limited resources.

An extended education provided topics for discussion, whereas those who could not fall back on such topics were deprived of the opportunity to converse. Trivial topics of general conversation, such as the deeds of the local football club, the weather, the actions of acquaintances, local living conditions, had no content in a POW camp in the jungle. Without such topics of conversation, the mind became dull, and interest in living was lost. It was observed that those who died had slowly become more silent and had lapsed into a state of lethargy.

There were other factors to be taken into consideration, such as whether the person had lived in a town or in the country. Those living in the country were more self reliant and adapted to what was, in effect, country living in a jungle. They expressed greater interest in their surroundings, which provided some exercise for their minds.

The ability to keep alive depended very much on personal hygiene, and here the regular soldiers had an advantage over the conscripts in the army. Ingrained habits from army life were followed by the regulars, even under the most adverse conditions. The attempt to be presentable by looking after cleanliness and clothes helped to maintain good health.

Lastly there was a factor that had nothing to do with mental activity or habit, it was simply a question of food. People of large stature needed more food than people of small stature, so the smaller, more wiry persons had a better chance of survival because all received the same inadequate rations. The rations could almost suffice for those of small stature, but were certainly inadequate for those of large stature and a starvation ration rendered a person more open to disease.

These factors were general trends and the death of some individuals caused us some surprise; there seemed to be no adequate reason for their inability to survive.

CHAPTER VIII

Pennies from heaven

T HE POWS IN THE CAMP at Tonchan South had now entered a much improved existence, mainly due to the purchase of food from the trading barges. I had been buying from these barges, using my knowledge of Thai, and now I was also buying for other camps in Tonchan near our own.

As our purchases had increased we used skips to collect the food. A skip was a basket woven from palm leaves and strengthened with bamboo; it was circular in shape with a diameter of about three feet and was about three and a half feet deep. To carry it, a bamboo pole was pushed through the top part of the skip, just below the rim, and the pole was carried on the shoulders of two people, with the skip between them.

Carrying loads in this fashion is a common practice in Asia. For heavy loads the skip with two men is employed. For lighter loads, a pole is carried on the shoulder by one man and the load consists of two parts, one at each end of the pole. The two loads are balanced at both ends by shifting the pole on the shoulder. The use of a pole for carrying heavy loads builds up a pad of muscle where the neck and shoulder meet. When carrying such a load we employed the method used by the local people. You walked with slightly bent knees, taking small steps, and grunting with every stride to avoid rupturing yourself with the weight.

Either two or four of us would set off in the morning to make our way down to the river. The path was hilly and care had to be taken if it was muddy and slippery. Having arrived at the river, I would go aboard the barges to see what each had to offer.

The most important purchase was fruit, because our diet lacked sweetness, and the barge traders had a good selection. I bought limes, Thai oranges which are very sweet, and bananas – usually the small, very yellow ones which are much sweeter than bananas bought in England. There were also pineapples and papayas, both sweet, and pomelos, the latter being like a large grapefruit, but less juicy and not so sweet as the other fruit.

For vegetables there were onions and garlic, both useful to flavour our stews, while Chinese radish and many types of green vegetables were also available. All these made the stews much more appetizing.

For protein I purchased duck eggs and generally bought one thousand at a time. These eggs were counted individually – which improved my counting in Thai considerably. With this buying of eggs went the purchase of oil for frying, usually coconut oil, which was available in tins. Each tin contained four gallons of coconut oil, so it had to be divided up into smaller amounts to be sold to individual members of the camp.

Everyone became expert at making omelettes from duck eggs, usually thickened with a little rice to make a substantial meal. The omelettes were flavoured with onions, garlic, or limes with added sugar.

For sugar I bought gula Malacca, palm sugar, which was brown in colour and similar to very thick treacle. It made an excellent omelette with limes. Palm sugar is prepared by tieing the flower at the top of a coconut palm at top and bottom. A slit is made in the enveloping leaves and the flower is beaten with a stick. This causes sap to exude from the flower, and this is then collected in a receptacle.

The receptacle is sterilized with a piece of slaked lime, otherwise the sap ferments and toddy, a very alcoholic drink, is formed. The sap is boiled and, on cooling, forms a treacle-like liquid or a soft, brown solid. Coconuts were also on sale but were not that popular with the troops.

The barges stocked Thai cigarettes which were expensive as far as we were concerned, but were excellent. A cheaper form of tobacco was sold in hanks, with an ounce of tobacco being about a foot square and two inches thick. It was very loose in texture and looked like dried grass, but was quite strong when smoked. The troops nicknamed it 'hag's bush'. Paper could be purchased to roll cigarettes.

We could also buy a few luxuries such as soap, a sarong, a good pair of sandals – provided we had the money – but usually food came first.

The accountant and I ran a canteen where all ranks could purchase what they could afford. This needed some choice to be made because the pay would not stretch to everything a person would have liked to buy. The canteen was run at a profit to purchase food, and other odd amenities, for the sick in hospital. They still received neither food nor pay, and though we could manage to give them the standard rations from the rations for the whole camp, the extra food was welcome.

Clothing was still short and I was reduced to a sarong, a pair of *teroma-pak*, the local wooden sandals, and my trilby hat – quite a distinctive costume. I was also becoming well known on the barges as the traders were intrigued by a European speaking Thai.

When buying goods out East conversation starts in a general fashion. There are the usual questions 'Are you married?' 'How many children do you have? – the latter question being asked irrespective of whether one is married or not. Questions are asked about where you live, how much ground you have, and what kind of house do you live in, all difficult questions to answer against a Thai background. When such questions are finished, haggling over the price of goods can commence.

The same kind of questions could also be posed by Japanese soldiers. The guards would ask POWs when they were working 'You *wifu-kah*' that is 'have you a wife?' If you said no and wore glasses you were likely to get your face slapped. According to the Japanese married men were supposed to wear glasses, but bachelors were not supposed to wear them. We never found out why.

One barge was owned by a young Thai woman, who we all thought was one of the prettiest women we had ever seen. Perhaps that was due to the fact we had not seen any other woman for some considerable time. However, we discovered later that Thai women have a reputation for being beautiful.

She was christened Lulu and I tended to do most of my trading with her. She became very friendly and after I had made my purchases, she would give me a gift of food. This was often a Thai delicacy, some of which were strange to Western tastes, but one dish I came to like was fish fried with sugar, the fish being of the dried variety and possessing a rather gamey taste. For very large purchases Lulu would produce a bottle of Thai whisky, a lethal drink after many months of abstinence, but none the less very enjoyable. If I came with only one helper to carry the goods, then he would be invited aboard too, and enjoy her hospitality. To have this treatment was lucky indeed, as few other POWs could have been so fortunate – and it was all due to learning Thai.

The original reason I had learnt Thai arose when I had been joined in Changi by a friend, Bill Adams, who had been in the same regiment in England. We had gone out together by boat to India, but when we arrived in Bombay he was sent to Malaya to join the staff in Malaya Headquarters, and I was posted to the North-West Frontier in India.

After the capitulation of Singapore he came to join the regiment in the 11th Indian Division area and one day suggested to me that we might try to escape. In order to do so we had to pass through Malaya and Thailand, and then find our way through Burma. He suggested I learnt Malay and Thai so that we would stand a better chance of making our way through the different countries.

Bill started to teach me Thai; he had lived and worked in Thailand for ten years. I continued with the lessons in the Australian area of Changi. Malay I learnt in the 11th Indian Division area; we had several officers there who had previously worked in Malaya and had joined units both as interpreters and to provide local knowledge of the country .

My friend was sent to Thailand with a contingent of POWs before I went to live in Changi village. I eventually saw him in the distance when I was at Kanchanaburi, but we did not have a chance to talk.

I did not meet Bill again until I had returned to England and joined the Far East POW Club. I spent some time with him prior to leaving for Malaya to take up an appointment in the Colonial Civil Service in the middle of 1946. Although we chatted a lot about POW days, he never told me what he had really been doing in Thailand, and it was only in the nineties that I had a fuller realization of his experiences.

Rations had improved slightly because the railway was providing better transport to our camps; there were additional vegetables for the gascape stew. The Japanese headquarters had obviously decided that the rations must be improved to keep the POW from falling sick, so they sent up local cattle which were called yaks by the troops. These were the humped-back Indian variety, smaller than English cattle, and with thin legs.

A herd of yaks would pass by the camp practically every day, but none stopped to be given to our camp. The *gunso* must have inquired why we did not receive any cattle. He told me that, because we were part of the Singapura group, we were not going to get any. As we did not get yaks, neither did our guards.

The *gunso* suggested that we ought to try and catch a few yaks for our own use. I agreed and we formed a party of three, the *gunso* and two POWs. The *gunso* would hold the guards and the men herding the cattle in conversation and we would rustle one or two yaks. Sometimes the herd was stretched out over such a large distance that there was no need for the *gunso* to hold the guards and herdsmen in conversation and we could steal two or three yaks without being noticed.

The yaks had to be hidden from prying eyes, so we took them into the jungle where they had plenty to eat. When they arrived at our camp they were very thin from being driven a long distance from the coastal plain. Hiding them in the jungle gave them a chance to fatten up.

As soon as we had four or five fattened up we killed and ate the first one. The meal – with the first meat we had eaten for a year and a half – was delicious. Naturally we had to bribe the guards with the best parts of the carcase, but the rest of the meat was excellent.

The guards were enjoying the meat as much as we were, and so they kept the rustling secret; we built up a herd which reached fifteen. One yak, a cow with only one horn, was the leader of the herd, and the *gunso* managed to get a bell to tie on her. She kept the herd together and we could hear the bell when she was wandering in the jungle, to locate it. The jungle in the hill above the camp was not thick, more like an English wood, so locating the yak was not too difficult. After killing and eating an animal the remains had to be carefully buried so that no one would suspect we were getting meat.

We were lucky that our camp appeared to have been forgotten by the Japanese, since nobody came to inspect us and thus discover a yak being cooked. The meat in the diet gave the men renewed vigour and no doubt helped many to survive their further experiences in Thailand.

When herding the cattle we explored the jungle. There was a stream which flowed down to the River Kwai and the water in it was crystal clear.

Those herding the cattle would bathe in this stream as we thought it was safe from infection. It came straight out of the jungle and flowed down from the hill with no habitation near it and no possibility of contamination from human beings.

At that stage of our captivity we had not heard of leptospirosis, called Japanese river fever in Malaya. It is a disease spread by rats' urine, and before the discovery of antibiotics, was usually fatal. There are plenty of rats in the jungle and it was probable that most rivers and streams would be contaminated with the spirochaetes of leptospirosis. Luckily we did not know about leptospirosis and, in our ignorance, bathed happily.

Keeping still while tending the herd of yaks so as not to disturb them feeding, we observed many jungle creatures. The most fantastic were the lizards, creatures about a foot long, with the most vivid green and red coloration I have ever seen. They had crests along their backs and looked like small prehistoric dinosaurs. Basking in the sun they could be observed lying on the many limestone rock outcrops in the jungle.

There was the odd snake to be seen, but lizards were in the majority. There may have been larger animals, but animals such as the big cats do not hunt in the daytime, and we were always back in camp well before dusk. The smaller animals, such as rats, were rarely sighted.

One day some high ranking Japanese officers came to visit the camps and the railway. The *gunso* was very busy with them and one evening explained to me that they wanted to make some purchases from the Thai traders.

The next day I duly assembled the traders and we met the Japanese officers. We sat in the shape of the letter U, with the Japanese sitting tailor fashion down one side of the U and the Thai traders squatting, facing them on the other side of the U. The *gunso* sat by the Japanese officers and I sat by the Thais to complete the letter U.

The Japanese would make a request which the *gunso* translated into Malay to me and then I translated the Malay into Thai for the traders. The answer went back in the reverse direction in all three languages – a laborious business. The officers were wanting fruit and other things that the Thais could supply, so the whole proceedings passed off satisfactorily; the Thais traded without too much haggling over price.

The Japanese were obviously pleased and complimented the *gunso*. He in turn showed us his appreciation with some extra gifts that night. It was a strange experience and could have gone badly wrong because the Thais were not over fond of the Japanese.

The advent of the high ranking officers puzzled us for a while but the reason for the visit soon came clear. They were obviously considering the state of progress of the railway and had decided that it was now complete up to Tonchan.

Although their presence could be explained by this decision it did not explain their wish to buy goods from the Thai traders at our particular camp. As far as I knew, they would have had as much success at any one of the other local camps.

Looking at the eposode in hindsight, perhaps word had filtered through to the higher echelons in Bangkok that Tonchan South was a well organized camp, with trading facilities. The reputation of the *gunso* for maintaining a trouble-free camp could also have been part of the information. This aspect of the visitation may have been nearer the truth than I thought, because, at a later date, when I met Oburi again, he had been promoted.

There was no doubt that Oburi *gunso* had given considerable help to all POWs in Tonchan South. The improvement in rations, mainly due to getting meat, the treatment of skin complaints, and the lessening of interference from the guards, had all contributed to improving the troops' spirits, and thus helped them to survive the hazards of POW life

The camps at Tonchan we learnt were only temporary, and were to be dismantled when this section of the railway was considered finished; they were the only temporary sites.

The decision was now taken that the section was finished and we were given orders to move on up country, having dismantled the camp.

CHAPTER IX

A slow boat to Burma

THE CAMP AT TONCHAN SOUTH was now closed down. The tents and camp equipment were taken down to the river and loaded by stages on to a barge, until little remained. The *gunso* told me to go with the barge and take one other POW. I chose a Dutchman who had come from Java; I thought he would be useful up country to sort out any problems, being better acquainted with jungle conditions than I was. Of mixed Javanese and Dutch descent, he had been a minor government official in Java. Having also been a sergeant in an infantry regiment he proved himself of great use on the barge.

The orders from the Japanese headquarters were that the *gunso* would march up the road from camp to camp and the barge would go up the river, meeting the road party at each camp. The barge was towed by a small launch in which were four guards with orders where they had to report. It was loaded with rations for the road party as well as with the tents and equipment.

The barge was large, about fifty feet long by ten or so feet wide and built of teak – a good solid construction. At the stern was a platform for the steersman to hold the rudder to guide the towed barge. Above this platform was a wooden canopy, providing shade for the steersman.

Just in front of the platform was a hatch-way down to a cabin with a semicircular roof. In this cabin lived the Thai barge owner and his family, consisting of his wife and two small children. In front of this cabin, the semicircular roof was continued to cover a hold in which were the stores.

The roof did not reach to the sides of the barge; a narrow gangway allowed passage from the stern to the bows of the boat. This gangway was about one foot wide, and there were no hand-holds on the roof, so it needed a steady foothold.

Entrance to the hold was at the front of the barge and from floor boards to the roof in the middle of the hold was about six feet. The bows had a triangular platform from which one stepped down into the hold; all the loading of the barge took place from this platform.

On the front platform was a post to which was tied the rope for towing, and just behind the post was a small hatch from which it was possible to get into the forepeak of the boat and inspect the bows. At the front of the back platform – just behind the entrance to the family cabin – was a baulk of timber, part of the deck, that projected over the sides of the boat. On each side was a shallow hole into which the cooking equipment for the barge was put.

These cooking utensils consisted of a circular earthenware vessel with a space underneath for a charcoal fire and above this a pot with a lid – all one piece of pottery. The space for the fire had a hole at one point of its circumference. When the barge was moving this hole was pointing backwards, but the vessel could be turned to face the bows and thus increase the draught from the wind to fan the fire.

All the meals were cooked in two pots, one on each side of the barge. One pot held rice and the other the main part of the meal. Food could be fried or boiled in the pots in the way described for making a *bah mee* when we were at Tarsao. The pots were also used to boil water for washing, so that both the Thais and ourselves could wash in clean water.

The barge has been described in some detail because we were going to live on it for a long trip which lasted for ten or more days. It was also of interest because many Thai families live in this way on boats on the numerous rivers and *klongs** in the country.

The launch used by the guards was an interesting adaptation of river craft. It consisted of three sections: a bow section, an oblong section, and an engine and steering section, all made of steel. The sides of all sections were of the same height; each was complete in itself and would float unaided.

The three sections were bolted together to form the launch. Other launches could be made by adding one or more oblong sections, so craft of different sizes could be made for any particular purpose. The only essential was that each had to have a bow and an engine section.

We were now ready to start our journey from Tonchan South, and set off late in the morning, at the same time as the road party started to march up country. I did not envy them as I was bound for a much more leisurely journey. We had no idea how far they were going to march because we had no knowledge of our destination.

The tide was fairly strong so the speed of towing was slow. We tied up for the night and the Thai family cooked the first meal and ate it with us; it was a pleasant change from camp cooking. Our rations included Number 1 fish, which the Thais had dried in the sun as we moved up river. This was turned into a mixture with vegetables and rice, flavoured with onions, garlic and other herbs. Like the Thais we ate with our fingers from a small bowl and drank the liquid portion of the meal.

There was nothing for the Dutchman and me to do as we progressed up the river, other than to sit up in the bows and watch the countryside go by. We had three meals a day, morning, noon and evening, all cooked by the barge owner's wife. Travelling in this leisurely way we reached our first port of call at Hin Tok and waited for the road party to catch us up.

We were not allowed off and a fatigue party from the road contingent came to collect rations from the barge. When the road party set off next day we moved off at the same time. It was obvious that we were going to be

---

* A *klong* can best be described as a canal running through settled areas as well as countryside.

much quicker than those who were marching, and this proved to be the case at each stop.

The guards were also enjoying their relaxation from normal duties. Some of them tried fishing from their launch, although I did not see them catch anything. They had their own rations and were not dependent on the barge for food. After two or three days they had relaxed enough to give us their rifles for cleaning – although they wisely kept the ammunition on the launch. Apart from an occasional command, we hardly communicated with the guards.

We put in at various camps as we continued our trip up river, for many of which we did not find out the name. At each stop we saw Thai trading barges, obviously doing a roaring trade with the camp guards and probably the POWs too. Some of the camps had many barges, so there must have been large contingents of guards and prisoners.

Both we and the Thai family traded with the barges for food. Here the Dutch sergeant proved invaluable as he knew the local produce and other types of food. The Thais are fond of fermented shellfish products, such as powdered prawns dried in the sun and buried in sand for a few months to enhance the flavour.

Such specialities I enjoyed when fried – but boiled and added to a noodle dish, I found them hard to stomach. So the Dutch sergeant watched over the purchases from the traders and selected the types of food that Europeans liked. This allowed me to enjoy all the meals on the barge. By this time we no longer saw our own troops coming to the barge to collect rations. We tried to inquire where they were, but received no answer.

We put in at one camp where there was a large cantilever bridge. There we stayed for some time and I managed to talk to the POWs who came to the barge to collect stores.

The place, I think, was called Tamaran Park – probably the anglicisation of the Thai name, Tamarkan. I gathered that there had been an officers' working party at this camp who had disagreed with the Japanese engineers on the way to build the bridge. Somehow the British officers had persuaded the Japanese to let them take over the planning and building but when the bridge was near completion it had collapsed, and the Japanese had had to erect it again. The bridge had been nicknamed Shoko's Folly, *shoko* being the Japanese for officer. When, later on, I travelled by rail back down the river route, I remembered Shoko's Folly, and hoped the bridges over which we went had been made secure

Some of the camps were right down by the river. Others that we could not see were higher up, depending on the actual route of the railway. The huts in all these camps were made of bamboo sides with palm leaf thatch, and some looked in good condition, while others looked in poor shape.

Each camp was responsible for building a section of the railway, and when their task was completed the rail-laying company came through – as it did at Tonchan – to lay the rails on the embankments built by the POWs. The section at Tonchan must have been an easier section than elsewhere; the camps in that area were not permanent as were the camps we were now visiting.

Half way up the river we picked up an Australian soldier, who was put on the boat without any explanation. This caused trouble with the Thai family. The Dutch sergeant and I had followed the custom of Thailand and did not wear shoes or any kind of footwear on the barge. It is usual in Asia, at least the tropical parts of it, to take off one's shoes when entering a house or any other kind of living accommodation. This ensures that no dirt contaminates the house and keeps down the incidence of disease. All floors are spotlessly clean and wearing one's shoes would make a person feel guilty of sullying the domestic conditions. The floors are often made of polished teak, in all but the poorest homes, and are polished until they shine. Walking on them with dirty shoes quickly ruins the beautiful surface.

The barge was kept immaculate by the barge owner; while he was cleaning the barge his wife was steering. The boards of the deck were swept and polished every day, so it was annoying to see the Australian refusing to remove his shoes. He said he was not going to behave like any bloody Boong – so the Dutch sergeant and I had to remove his shoes forcibly.

On questioning him I found out that he had not washed for several months because cholera had stopped all washing unless boiled water could be obtained. I believed him; he stank and his skin was covered in small pustules. He was a very unprepossessing sight.

I banned him from coming aft to meet the Thai family because they obviously did not like him at all. In this I was grateful for the presence of the Dutch sergeant, a man who looked as if he would brook no trouble.

The peace of the barge's voyage had now been broken, as I had to watch out for friction between the Thais and the Australian. This was a pity because the voyage was proving very interesting. Few Europeans had probably made such a voyage and I was fascinated by the river traffic and the different aspects of the country through which we were passing.

The whole trip up the river was about one hundred and fifty miles – which accounts for the road party not keeping up with the barge. A march of this length under tropical conditions, with poor food, was weeding out those who were unfit. We presumed that those who fell sick were left behind at the various camps on the route.

After more than one week of working our way up river the Thai boatman started to look worried and was continually examining the bows of the barge. Although we made slow progress in distance travelled, the river was

ance in the camp. This was a very welcome sight, but the distribution left a lot to be desired; it worked out at about one parcel per fifteen persons. While the parcels were appreciated, they produced problems such as how to divide a half-pound slab of chocolate between fifteen men. A strict division pro rata would mean losing a part of the chocolate in the division and each man's portion would be too small either to enjoy or even to see.

The problem was solved initially by putting every item into cakes, pies, or other culinary efforts and then dividing the offering into fifteen portions. Unfortunately, the group to which I belonged had seventeen persons and, as I was a scientist, I had the task of dividing the cake or pie into seventeen portions. With a round cake this is difficult, but with a rectangular cake it is almost impossible. I attempted the task, carefully watched by sixteen pairs of calculating eyes, eager to see a slip and make capital out of it.

The parcels did not arrive that often, maybe one every two or three weeks, and then the task of division would arise. After several nerve-racking divisions of cakes and pies I suggested an alternative. I would divide the cake or pie into twenty-four pieces, everyone would get his share and seven lucky people would get two shares.

A roster would then be established and would move down the seventeen each time we had a share out. This was accepted as a good idea, and we cut cards for the order of the roster. The next step was how to record the roster. One member had the bright idea of using a cribbage board, numbered against the roster, with four rosters for different categories, such as one for sweet cakes, one for savoury pies, one for sweets or similar countable offerings, and one for cigarettes.

The system worked magnificently and all were happy. There was an element of chance in the draw, depending on the contents of the Red Cross parcel, but this made it more exciting and something to look forward to in what was otherwise a monotonous existence.

However, one day tragedy struck. A clumsy member of the seventeen-man group dropped the cribbage board and all the pins fell out. There was consternation and furious arguments as to where the pins had been when the accident happened. The matter was finally settled, but one or two members of the group were not on speaking terms for several weeks after the incident.

This method of giving any excess food to people on a roster was used by all the cookhouses, and it was known as the 'leggy queue', the word 'leggy' being a corruption from the Malay word *lagi* which means 'more in addition' as opposed to 'more than' as in more than two hundred. Our cribbage board was known as the leggy board.

When we were in the huts around the gaol, the whole camp, gaol and huts was under the command of a Japanese lieutenant whose name was

Takahashi. He lived outside the camp and employed POWs to maintain his house and compound. He had a very pretty Malay mistress, with whom he apparently was deeply in love. To show his affection he decided to build a pleasure pavilion of the type common in the East.

A fortunate site must always have 'good wind and water' so the pavilion was built on stilts out in the sea beyond low tide, with a bridge leading from the land to the pavilion. The troops working on this project were mainly Australians, and they took their time over the work in hand. It was pleasant work and they saw no need to hurry it. Eventually the pavilion was finished and Takahashi and his mistress enjoyed their new surroundings.

In the meantime the Malay girl had become pregnant and Takahashi was proud of his prowess. The infant was duly born and then there was trouble; the infant was obviously Eurasian. Takahashi was furious and demanded to know who was responsible, but everybody remained silent. Not finding the culprit, Takahashi showed his displeasure by stopping the cigarette ration of the POWs for one month. This was serious news indeed, and if we had found the culprit, who we strongly believed was an Australian, he would have been lynched.

Early on in spring 1945 I was put in charge of a hut containing one hundred men. The hut was the first one near the perimeter fence, bordering on the road on the west side of the gaol. I nominated the men for working parties to see that all had a fair chance of working and getting paid. I did not go out on any of these parties, but remained in camp to oversee the hut.

One day Lieutenant Takahashi was summoned to Tokyo and faced a problem. Since giving up his Malay mistress he had adopted a monkey. He could not take the monkey with him and he did not trust anyone in his quarters to look after the monkey, so he decided to leave it in the charge of one of the POWs. As I was nearest to the perimeter wire, he thought this gave the monkey the best chance of living, so it was put in my charge.

This was a terrific responsibility, remembering the loss of the cigarette ration for the failure of his mistress to reserve herself for Takahashi. It was a greater responsibility than most realised, because the men in the camp were very hungry and any chance of a meat meal was very tempting. I deputed three men to be in charge of the monkey, and inspected the guardians every few hours. I insisted they slept with the monkey tied to their waists because otherwise the monkey would certainly be lost to a passing thief.

At that time there were several pets in the camp, especially dogs. Anybody who owned a dog also slept with it tied to his waist. so that he was aware of any attempt to steal it. A stray dog walking by a hut would be skinned and in the pot within ten minutes; the camp inhabitants were very hungry.

The monkey was thus carefully guarded as I did not wish her to end up in

146

a stew. My arrangements worked satisfactorily and I was relieved to hand the monkey back to Takahashi on his return from Tokyo. But during the period of guarding the animal I had had a lot of time to study the antics of monkeys. The monkey was a female – there was nothing queer about Takahashi – and so clung to her male guards. I do not think a male monkey would have survived the experience. She was greedy, wily, and playful, and we became fond of her, and almost sorry to say goodbye.

When I took up the position of being in charge of the hut, I was transferred to a new mess. I moved in and awaited my first meal. To my surprise the senior officer asked 'Are you one of those officers with caliper eyes?' This I could hardly deny; like all POWs I could gauge the size of any dish with great accuracy. So I could only reply 'Not more so than most of the people in camp'.

News of the Allied landings in Europe had given us a new lease of life and a desire to catch up on the years being wasted in captivity. Courses were started for anybody who wished to participate. Academic courses were available up to university standard.

I took part in chemistry courses and lectured on the subject, using the books available in the library. Paper was in short supply, which reduced any work on a subject to oral presentation. I enjoyed the mental stimulation of having to prepare a lecture or talk and the students had the satisfaction of knowing that they were preparing themselves for work after liberation.

News was now plentiful, and the organization for its dissemination was as near foolproof as was possible. I attended a group of POWs with one person giving an account of the BBC news bulletin every day. This I had to learn by heart and, by the end of the stay in Changi, most of us could hear and repeat accurately a full twenty minutes of reported news.

I then went to another group where I was the dispenser of news and the others digested the report and learnt it. This procedure was repeated and I was also a member of another group, so I could check on the accuracy with which the news was being passed down the line of communication. The organization for dispensing the news was based on the principle of the communist cells. If any one person was interrogated and gave away the name of the news spokesman, that spokesman, in turn, would give the name of his spokesman, but the Japanese would go round and round the various overlapping circles. It would be almost impossible to locate the actual head of the cell network.

Details of the naval battles in the Pacific Ocean were remembered with great accuracy and I was surprised how little variation there was by the time I attended my second news group. The news of the Japanese war obviously interested us more than the news on the European fronts, and we followed the island-hopping campaign in the Pacific with great interest – at the same time vastly improving our knowledge of geography.

It was not until I returned to England and had been home for about two months that I discovered the source of the news in the Changi Gaol camp. The original source was one of the students to whom I taught chemistry, so probably I was in the very first group to receive the news. Presumably, there must have been a few senior officers who had instigated the reception of news and the cell organization for spreading it.

The radio operator slept on a *charpoy*, an Indian bed with four thick legs, each about six inches square, and a framework on which a string net provided the bed. The radio was hidden in one of the legs and was operated by a switch which was a knot in the wood. Another knot was exactly in front of a loudspeaker, and to listen in to the radio the operator held a stethoscope to the knot. The radio was completely disguised and only the actual sight of the operator using the stethoscope would have revealed it.

The Japanese were aware that news was filtering through to the POWs because there was an undercurrent of wellbeing when the news was good and the converse when the news was either poor or uninteresting. Surprise searches of the huts were conducted, both by day and by night, to try to catch the radio operator, but never succeeded.

Although the news was improving as the days went on, the war was obviously still a long way from reaching Singapore or anywhere near it. The Japanese were in control of the whole of modern Indonesia, and the nearest fighting to us was in the Andaman Islands. The landing at Leyte in the Phillipines gave us hope that the war was coming our way, but then Allied forces turned away and headed for Okinawa, leaving us out of the strategic advance.

The fighting in Burma was getting near Rangoon but there seemed little hope of the XIVth Army reaching Malaya for some considerable time.

CHAPTER XVI

Confucius – he say

FROM MY VANTAGE POINT in the hut near the perimeter wire I could see that the transport arriving at the gaol was becoming scarcer and all vehicles were now using the large cylinders generating gas from charcoal. The petrol shortage was getting severe and this had the effect of reducing the amount of food supplied to the camp.

The rice ration was reduced to five ounces per man per day, which is less than the normal requirement for an individual. The supply of vegetables was reasonable, being supplemented by produce from the gardens maintained by the POWs, and we were being issued with more fish. The two useful items of fish were shark and giant ray; shark makes an excellent meal, as does ray; both are cartilaginous fish with firm, solid flesh.

Giant rays arrived whole at the camp. The fish were diamond shape, about six feet long by about five feet wide, with a corresponding thickness of flesh. They had very long tails – I estimated up to twenty feet long – with a nasty looking barb at the end. The fish were cut up in the camp, and distributed to the cookhouses.

With the shortness of rations everybody dreamt of food; it was also in our thoughts whenever we were awake. Along with others, I used to talk to people who had spent their lives out East, about the various oriental dishes and the way of cooking them. I even remember with delight the recipe for fried duck skin. All these words of culinary information were written down on odd scraps of paper, hopefully for use when we were freed.

The experience of semi-starvation caused us to be determined that we would never go hungry again. We all decided that, on our return to England, we would indulge in four square meals a day. Food became an obsession, and we learnt to hate the thought of food being wasted. With this view went the accompanying thought that water should not be wasted, and I – and I think most other POWs – could not bear to see a tap running without the water being used. However long ago we experienced the shortage of food and water, the two hatreds of waste exist still today, personally speaking, and I think all ex-POWs would be in agreement.

The Japanese had issued a currency for Malaya, with notes for all denominations, the unit being a dollar, divided into one hundred cents. There were even notes for denominations for cents, not that such notes would buy much. The characteristic feature of the notes was a banana tree on each side of the bank-note, and the money was derisively called 'wang pisang' in Malay, which is 'banana money'. The notes were easy to forge and rumour had it that many Chinese had a printing press in a back room and were churning out the bank-notes like confetti.

We gathered later that the British government had helped in this process of increasing the supply of money, by flooding the country with bank-notes dropped from aeroplanes to the guerrilla troops in the jungle. Whoever was responsible for all the extra money, the result was inflation on a scale unimaginable. When we first entered Changi a coconut cost four cents; it now cost fifty-five dollars, so a small share of a coconut was all that could be managed from our pay each month

Tobacco cost thirty-five dollars an ounce, and cigars and cigarettes were well beyond our spending power. Two or three POWs would club together to buy an ounce of tobacco and then share it amongst them. We adopted the Chinese method of rolling a cigarette with the paper in the form of a cone, the apex being placed in the mouth, so that as little tobacco as possible was wasted at the end of a smoke. The experience of inflation in Singapore stayed with us for a long time and even now is one of the frightening thoughts of present life.

There was a little spare ground in the camp area near the huts, and some POWs managed to keep chickens, closely guarded, as the eggs were an important supplement to the diet. One day a friend invited me to a chicken curry. I was surprised, because I thought he had given up keeping chickens. He said he hadn't, so late in the evening along I went to his hut, and joined some others for the chicken curry.

The curry was delicious and I enjoyed every mouthful. When I had finished I was chatting to one of the others who had also enjoyed the meal, and asked him where the chickens were now being kept. He replied 'We gave up keeping chickens last month, it wasn't chicken, it was rat'. I immediately felt uncomfortable and rushed out and vomited. I was furious with myself at losing all that good protein, but the thought of eating rat was just too much, however hungry I felt.

The spices for the curry had come from the black market; several of the POWs were escaping through the wire at night and buying food and other goods from the Chinese in the vicinity. This was a dangerous occupation, because if caught, the penalty could be severe.

The men engaged in the black market had started business by selling their personal belongings, such as watches, Parker pens, and rings, to the guards, who were always on the lookout for Rolex watches and goods of similar quality. Those men who had begun in the black market, had contacted agents in Singapore town through the local Chinese, who had continued to live in their villages and hamlets within the main perimeter wire of Changi camp.

Through these agents, local produce was available – at a price. Popular items were *Ikan bilis*, a kind of whitebait – a good source of protein and calcium – which cost about thirty-five dollars a pound, and *belachan* which was dried prawn paste. *Belachan* is made by pounding small shrimps into a paste, wrapping the paste in palm leaves and burying the bundle in sand on the sea shore for several months. The resultant flavour is that of cheese mixed with rotten fish.

The *belachan* is fried and mixed with rice; our mouths would water if we smelt it frying. As a flavouring for rice, *belachan* was excellent, but after the war was over, I no longer fancied it. This shows how much hunger affects one's taste in food. Extra items of food, such as those described, were cooked on individual fires in the prison compound

Some of the black marketeers were willing to change cheques for banana money, with the highest rate of exchange at two banana dollars to a pound sterling. Even at this rate it was occasionally worthwhile to get some money by issuing a sterling cheque, because you were never sure that you would return to the UK to enjoy the balance accumulating in your bank account.

There were a few working parties going to Singapore for the purpose of clearing up areas which needed maintenance. One of these working parties was busy near the dock area of Singapore when there was a daylight air raid. The men in the working party saw American B29 bombers attacking the harbour, with the bombs causing damage in the harbour area. On their return to Changi we had a first hand report of the air raid.

This air raid was some time in early summer 1945, and we waited impatiently for it to be reported on the news. But the raid was not mentioned and we realized that Malaya was not very high on the priority of the media – or on the Allies plans of attack – in South East Asia. Yet it was the first indication that Malaya was a target, even if a minor one, and gave us hope that the war in the East was speeding up.

Working parties now went to clear up the bomb damage. The Chinese population was also cheered by the raid, and the local inhabitants were becoming more friendly as they could see that the Japanese were probably going to be defeated.

All POWs were warned not to mention any reference to the war when Japanese troops were about, just in case they should understand what was under discussion. Any reference to the Japanese government was disguised by reference to the Emperor, called '*Tenno Haika*' in Japanese – as far as one could guess the correct pronunciation and spelling of a name not seen in print. The initials TH were transformed into Toc H, an allusion to the Christian group formed during the First World War.

Any reference to the Japanese was given as Toc H, so any Japanese listening to a conversation and inquiring about the subject under discussion would be told it was about religion. As the Japanese respected religions of all kinds, such an answer removed any suspicion of the discussion. The news from Europe was now improving every time we listened to a bulletin. We

151

heard that the Allies had crossed the Rhine and invaded Germany. We listened to the description of the fall of Berlin, and probably knew more about it than many people in the UK, because we were repeating the news verbatim by this time, having had so much practice.

The report of VE day was a cause for rejoicing, as we realized that the whole of the Allied effort would now be turned on Japan. The action was getting nearer, with the American assault on the islands in the Phillipines, but those islands were about two thousand miles away from Singapore.

The Japanese must have heard about the fall of Germany, because Takahashi, the camp commandant, was making allusions to the war. Such information spread rapidly throughout the camp, and his cryptic remarks became known as 'Takahashi – he say'. Reference to the difficulties of surrender by the Japanese came as the Chinese proverb, 'He who rides the tiger cannot dismount'. An attempt to be friendly would appear as another Chinese saying, 'Beneath the four seas all men are brothers'. Takahashi obviously realized the war was approaching an end – with defeat for Japan – and he appeared to be building up goodwill between himself and the POWs. He could not go too far with his friendliness because his superiors were not of like mind. There was a general feeling of restlessness in the camp, with liberation appearing almost in our grasp. This feeling was enhanced by the news of the celebrations in Britain, and accompanied by doubts as to whether the fighting out East would be forgotten in the relief at the war ending in Europe.

We knew that the XIVth Army in Burma had been called 'The Forgotten Army' and suspected we might be the forgotten theatre of war. In June the news came that an attack had been made by Australian forces on Balikpapan, on the west coast of Borneo. There were oil wells there and we could see that the Allies were attempting to deny oil supplies to the Japanese. Balikpapan was also only about five hundred miles from Singapore, so war activity was coming closer.

The Australian forces next landed in British North Borneo, now called Sabah. The delight at hearing this news was tempered by the information about the POWs there; two contingents had gone from the regiment to Borneo early in 1943. We had been informed of their destination by the Japanese, so I had a personal interest in the news. When the Australians landed, the POWs in Sabah were taken on a forced march to prevent them being released by the attacking force. Many had died from this forced march and the remainder had eventually been released when the Australians caught up with the Japanese.

Our position in Singapore was then considered carefully. Where could we be forced to march from Singapore, if a landing was made on the island? If the mainland was attacked, would we be taken off in boats? We had heard on the news, months before, that several ships containing POWs bound for Japan had been sunk, and the prisoners on board had all been drowned.

After the landings on Borneo the news became quiet, and we were left wondering where the next assault would be. Then one day, two Allied planes flew over the camp. They were identified as Lightnings, with apparently two fuselages leading to two tail planes and with the cockpit in a nacelle between the fuselages. The planes flew over the camp, circled round it and then flew off. This was a cheering sight; the Australians now knew where the POW camp was located and we hoped it would not be bombed as a Japanese troop camp.

The Americans had been carrying out landings on the Japanese occupied islands of the Phillipines and they landed on an island called Palawan, the nearest island to the coast of Borneo.

The news of Okinawa and Iwojima had been of interest because the American forces were approaching the Japanese mainland. We hoped that the war out East would end with an attack on the mainland and with all the occupied areas in South East Asia then surrendering. This would be a safer bet for us to be released unharmed.

The news from Palawan, however, was the worst to date. When the American forces liberated the POW camp, they found that all the POWs had been burnt to death, and none had survived. Here was a second scenario for us to contemplate – march or burn. Perhaps it would have been better not to have heard the news; it only increased our anxieties.

One and all started to inspect the camp area very thoroughly, trying to make a plan for the various contingencies. The guards were too few to deal with the six or seven thousand prisoners in the camp, so presumably any Japanese troops in Singapore would be brought out to Changi to deal with the situation. The burning scenario was doubtful as it would entail all POWs concentrated in the gaol, and that would not burn very easily, being very solid stone.

So, on the whole, we thought that a march up country was going to be the answer, and we correspondingly made plans for an escape under such circumstances. Meanwhile, there was hardly any news of activity on any of the Eastern fronts. Burma was quiet, there was no further activity towards Japan, and Borneo seemed to have died down.

It was the middle of July and the war seemed to be suspended. The news came from Britain that Churchill had lost the election and that Britain now had a socialist government. This news was given a mixed reception, because most of us would have liked Churchill to keep on directing the British efforts to regain Malaya. The camp was in a state of suspended animation, not foreseeing the next direction of the war.

153